THE KEEPER'S VOICE

SOUTHERN MESSENGER POETS
Dave Smith, Series Editor

THE KEEPER'S VOICE

MIKE CARSON

poems

LOUISIANA STATE UNIVERSITY PRESS ❋ BATON ROUGE

Published by Louisiana State University Press
Copyright © 2010 by Mike Carson
All rights reserved
Manufactured in the United States of America
LSU Press Paperback Original

Designer: Amanda McDonald Scallan
Typeface: Trump Mediaeval

Library of Congress Cataloging-in-Publication Data
Carson, Mike, 1943–
 The keeper's voice : poems / Mike Carson.
   p. cm. – (Southern messenger poets)
 ISBN 978-0-8071-3618-8 (pbk. : alk. paper)
 I. Title.
 PS3603.A77623K44 2010
 811'.6–dc22
                                      2009053262

The author gratefully acknowledges the following journals in which some of these poems first appeared:

Amaryllis: "Honesty"
Beloit Poetry Journal: "Double"
The Evansville Review: "Castrating Shoats" (published as "Matter-of-Fact")
The Formalist: "Diver," "Kingfisher," "Of Soldiers and Others," "To My Wife Caring for Her Parents Far from Here"
The Hopkins Review: "Diagnosis," "Maggie"
Measure: "Just Weight," "No Surer Heaven," "Fullback," "The Keeper's Voice," "Etymology"
New Virginia Review: "Once His Hand"
The Southern Review: "Carrying"
Spoon River Quarterly: "Prophet," "Black Autumn"
Westview: "Muse"

Thanks to the University of Evansville for sabbatical leave to work on the poems in this collection.

The paper in this book meets the guidelines for permanence and durability of the Committee on Production Guidelines for Book Longevity of the Council on Library Resources. ∞

For Maggie

CONTENTS

1

Serving Early Mass in Winter 3
Castrating Shoats 5
Carrying 7
New Kid, St. James School 9
No Surer Heaven 11
Fullback 13
Etymology 15
Black Autumn 16
Double 18
Diver 20
"The Greatest Generation" 21
Indigo Bunting 23
Choir Boy 25

2

The Deal 29
Supper 30
Once His Hand 31
Muse 32
Kingfisher 34
Of Soldiers and Others 35
Box of Ashes 36
Honesty 37

Late Winter Night 38
The Fall 39
Prophet 40
Snake Handlers 41
Stoplight 42
Why Tom Kalen Rode the Bulls, and The Mystery
of the First Commandment 43

3

St. Matthew and the Angel 47

4

I'm Fine 55
Bloomington Landfill, Fourteen Degrees 56
Intention 57
The Sheep and the Goats 58
Keeping In Sight 59
Blue Note Lounge, Face-off 60
City Hospital, June Night 62
Christmas Weather Report 63
Diagnosis 64
To My Wife Caring for Her Parents Far from Here 65
Blue Nightgown 66
County Clare 67
Maggie 69
Just Weight 70
The Keeper's Voice 71

1

Love begins with remembering. . . . The poet must know, first, that the past is not only incomplete . . . but is capable of being completed.

—ANTONIO MACHADO
(*Antonio Machado: Selected Poems,* translated by Alan S. Trueblood)

Serving Early Mass in Winter

Who maketh his angels spirits;
his ministers a flaming fire
—PSALM 104

December, six a.m., the sidewalks buried,
Out of the dark the black biretta and cape
Of Father Dominic leans across the drifts.
"The padlock on the parking-lot gate has frozen,
You make a paper fire and thaw it out."

His army zippo solid as a gun
In my bare hand, I rip out, wad the pages—
The Indiana Catholic, Maryknoll,
Franciscan Way—light them, then feed in more.
The sudden yellow flames slash up, snap at
The wind that flails them, stars iced into the black,
The tears that freeze my lashes as I blink.

Beyond the pale lightfall of the church
I shiver, spread on pages that curl at once,
Gold snarls that eat the words, float off. How far
The back-row cop who kneels in uniform,
The hooded nuns, the whitehaired women praying,
Head-scarved, alone among the empty rows,
The *Introibo ad altare Dei,*
"I will go unto the altar of my God,"
Father mumbles, with no one to respond
Ad Deum qui laetificat, juventutem meam,
"To God who gives joy to my youth."

The lock and gate-bar blacken. The sisters
At Communion forget I'm here. The fire leaps
To twist out of itself. A distant heaven
Crowds close around the flame-light, fierce heat
I urge still higher—*St. Joseph Messenger,*

The Way, The Sacred Heart—thin newsprint wings
That open blazing, flap free above the gate.

Whole sheets of fire cut loose across the snow,
Catch empty bike racks, float through frozen chains
Of playground swings, then vanish on a hope,
Brief vision, into the darkened playing field.
One beats the fence, snuffs out. I'm down to scraps,
The fire-tongues shrink back. The prayers inside
Run down, the black print sinks in trembling ashflakes.

I warm the key above the dwindling fire,
It slides into the lock and clicks, the steel
Hinges screech open onto the untracked lot.
A few last shreds of light spawn small gray moths
That crumble, smudge the snow.
The prayer of fire gone, the Eucharist over,
Where shall I go? The heat inside the church
Is stale. The ice-glint stars fade into dawn.
The *Messengers* and *Ways* all gone in smoke.
Ite, Missa est. Go, the Mass is done.

Castrating Shoats

The first day water froze in the barnlot ruts
We cousins got to come, climb the haymow,
Bales stacked stories above the opening
That dropped into the feed racks, dirt-floored pen.
Up near the roof beams, the white-streaked swallow nests,
We tunneled, wrestled, leapt, ate dust, eye-stung
And wary of the sudden edge, the boss cat
That wrapped your leg and clawed and bit. The smell
Of clover stank so sweet we choked on it.
Below, young pigs came snuffling in. Our Uncle Bob
Looked up and called "Castrating shoats, get out."
No more than that, whatever it meant—not mean,
Just matter-of-fact. Outside, beyond the wall,
We played on, listening when we heard the squeals
That got into a rhythm that almost talked.
Till I could tell that they were scrambling
Stiff-legged, snouts up, climbing on each other's backs
To not get caught. I had a guess what caused
That riot of yipping grunts. Then at a shriek
I got a knothole glimpse, forelegs jerked up
By Uncle Jack, hindquarters hanging down
And spread. That pig's head nodded, guttural,
As if it had to find a way to talk.
And then its sound howled off and cauterized
Itself as those still left bunched, grumbling, down
Into a corner of the narrow pen.
Then the whole tribe chattered in strange tongues again.
My uncle was the kindest man I knew,
Yet he had sewed a sow's ears flapped across
Her eyes when she had taken to eating hens.
Not half so bad as Jesse Hiller though
Who'd stitched one's eyelids shut (what extra did
He mean by that?). I wanted all that day
To climb back high among the bales—what God

Did pigs belong to, not answering them?—to see
Myself the splattered shirts and chain-mail gloves,
But still keep playing, not exactly look.

Carrying

I didn't see it with my own eyes—hard to
Imagine—that Sunday noon, but soon
For an hour, the sun breaking in the trees,
I heard over and over the women,
My grandmother Marg especially, shrill
Maybe to scare me good, tell my heart how
The father, Den Harold, had carried her,
The dead body—himself—of the girl
Only five, Barbara, from where he had
Lifted her from our street, quiet, lined with
Big cars, two that she had, as he called her
To dinner, run between, into his cry.

That the tall man, white-shirted still from church,
Crossed from their porch, his name for her barely
Out of him, over the small yard, and stood
With her limp in his arms, and carried her
Looking exactly as she had to me—
Small face, the bob of her hair, her quick legs
Bare under her skirt, himself carry her.

Sunday noon had come empty in the street,
No one to bring her to him, so he moved
Her, in the women's talk, as he might have
Putting her in bed, disappeared over,
Over again into the house with her.
The words held us, seven and eight ourselves,
Tight into her guilt—forgetting to look—
As he walked with her in his arms and gone,
The car still in the street, the driver not
To blame, standing alone and crying, then
The prowl car, stopped and flashing, drawing out
Whole families from their meals, arranged on steps,
Close to each other, looking.

                                    And his own
Carrying told as if we could never
Name exactly enough into ourselves
What had happened, the word that she was now,
Said so surely that for years I thought I'd
Seen him cross the street, the way his head bowed,
His sleeves rolled up his outstretched arms, alone.
And so I weigh the child, put in my arms
The shape my grandmother gave to her love,
Say now the father—his name and care—
As he crosses the yard and I follow
In the shaded house we could not see into.
We lay the body in the quilted bed,
And I imagine as exactly as
I can that still she is and isn't dead.

New Kid, St. James School

It took two weeks for words to turn to fists,
Bloody shirts in the dusty playground lot
The nuns ignored at recess after lunch.
We could be friends then. I went to his house.

One knock, a chow-mutt crashes the door, is kicked
Aside. No mom in there, a dad as thick-
Backed as a hog, neck rippled up, bare skull.
Inside the door he sees me eye the dog.

To prove it loves him, how quick it will attack,
"Hit me, Tommy," he tells his son. "Go on."
Then from behind where he'd be hard to reach,
The kid draws back and slugs him in his neck.

The dog is snarling—a harder punch—darts out,
Snapping, then feinting in, can't know which leg
To clamp. The dad leans down behind and grabs
And shakes his own son's pants. "Here, boy," he growls,

The kid up on his toes and sledging shots,
Now double-fisted, meant to really connect.
They bounce off like a maul that hits a knot.
The dog is slobbering to bite, teeth bared, ears back,

It flinches at the hard-toed shuffling feet,
It starts to bite itself. "Enough, enough,"
Tom's old man straightens up, "goddammit, enough."
He turns and takes one last left hook that smacks.

The little brothers stop jumping on the couch,
Tom pushes up his glasses, tucks in his shirt.
Outside, a late-fall night, no sidewalks, no
Big streetlights by this rental house, its yard

All weeds that rattle in the settling dark.
I think I'd better leave, not sure how much
Whiskey the old man, now headed for the kitchen,
Has drunk. But then Tom grins, gives me a look,

I understand—why, in our fight when we
Were down and breathless, bloody-mouthed he cursed
In tears to keep me fighting him, till I
Just quit, no way I knew to hurt him worse.

No Surer Heaven

For Don Meyer

He taught me how to think the bullet in,
Along the flank behind the shoulder joint,
Or from the front, the line of crosshatched fur
That marks the heart upon the chest,
To not be smart and try and hit the brain
But always aim imagining the place
Behind the juncture in the bone, through ribs,
Snug in the softness of the lungs, the dark
Sung thing that I could picture even at ten.
As we sat silent against a tree, I looked
Till hand and eye were one, each made exact
Along the age-scarred, polished stock, dull gleam
Of blue-black metal, the tiny letters engraved—
A .22 Cal. Remington—outside
The chamber where the bullets sat tight in wait.
I lift the barrel, stare down the sight, steady
The bead into the notch, imagining
A knothole or a branch alive, the shot
Thought in through fur, through skin. It nicks the bone,
The emptied body lies in the leaves, my hand.

It's fifty years since he and I eased down
In Geren's Woods, his own heart years now gone—
So quiet and quick-eyed, kind to love a kid
Not his, by instinct never saying *I love*.
He put instead the rifle in my hands,
Gave me the name and use of all its parts.
And Sundays when my dad, hungover, slept,
Though no one asked him to he'd pick me up,
Take me to Lourdes for Mass to keep me safe
From mortal sin, I guessed. I had no prayer
But saw him kneel and knew his silence meant.
Beside him in the pew down near the front

Where votive candles burned in rows I dreamt
My separate dream, the trees high-arched and reaching through
The splays of sunlight sparkling with the wind,
The quiet they held because we listened for
The sound by which to sight the hidden one
That might come forth like Lazarus from the shadows
In the leaves—I hold my breath as he says to,
Think hard to squeeze the trigger slow. He is
A voice just out of sight, but close as prayer
To make me sure, to think the squirrel we'd skin,
And then at dinner, tasting hard, I'd eat.
At ten there is no heaven surer than
A loaded rifle in your hands, but when
He'd gone, left me alone to be a man,
I heard his words inside my own alive
Out in the woods again—*You get one shot,*
The true imagination of it. The heart,
And all he meant by that.

Fullback

The second poetry was locker room
. . . *the tough get going*, . . . *a quitter never wins*,
And on the field the words that gave it meat—
A forearm shiver, tuck it away and go.
What's said's so like the deed, adrenalin
We called *desire* made body thought, *crab block,
Crackback, dive play, trap left, straight arm, power sweep,*
The *ready-downset* shock held tight, *hut-hut,*
The snap and then the music in the smack
Of pads to orchestrate, sometimes with blood,
A blown-out knee—*clotheslined, sidelined, chimes rung*—
Into the twenty-two whose bodies rang,
Coldcocked, blindsided, Butch Kleppe, a hardnosed kid,
One Friday night flat on the field dead.

In his brief funeral silence we all thought
(The face still his, strong jawed, but not the wig
To hide the autopsy they put on him)
About what coach had said—*It's not the size
Of the dog in the fight . . . Keep your dobbers up*—
And listened hard between the lines for what,
Take it to 'em, make 'em pay, he had not.

Our words held ways to hit and take a hit.
What no one told you, son, when someone got
A shot at you and you went down and stayed
Each time a little longer, you were dying
And doing it alone. How could you guess?
You shook the headaches off, put on the pads,
The helmet not good enough, went out and knocked
Just that much tougher not to quit, the crowd
Forgot, while we proved words for sixty minutes
On Friday evenings under all that glare,
Not *gun shy* even when we saw you dead.

First poetry was *Requiem Aeternam*
Black vestments, candles, the dead march down the aisle
Into the songs, the *Dies Irae—day*
Of wrath and mourning trumpeted, by David,
By the Sybil's warning, the organ's haunting
The footfalls' pace, heads bowed, toward the grave,
The smoking censer signaling in ghosts,
Quantus tremor est futurus, felt first
In Latin, then half Englished in our need,
The souls cut out from time to wander doom,
Lux eternam dona eis, Domine.
Light eternal the most the unknown said.

Requiescat, Butch, fullback, in peace,
Run to daylight best chance we'd ever had.

Etymology

> "A *murder* of crows"

Late winter, crows flock thick near town, bend black
The branches of the firs outside this house.
One pair of them alone make deadly racket,
This brood of voices, not quite language, shrieks
Its cackling arguments. Then shouts for blood
I've never heard, I hear, this *murder* not,
As I had thought the term, the angry drunk
Dark-alleyed with his knife, no thug with need
And a gun, not husband or wife cheated to death
With grief to pay back, but a village cried up to mob
With stones and clubs even one of their own
Who's doing, who did, whatever the body could
Broken of rib and arm and head to fight back,
To twist out, give them their pleasure loud, till wet
Over the last of its groans, they looking askance
As birds in a settling flock, the soul had fled.

Whoever named this gathering knew well,
As those in whom the name caught on, the sound
Outside my wall today, "that hideous noise"
That Chaucer heard six hundred years before—
Jack Straw's plague troops that "yelled as fiends in hell . . .
When they would any Fleming kill." The same
Rank congregation of tongues that squawked Christ's death
And haled Jim Crow to a lynching in the woods,
Blasphemed the streets with rocks on Kristallnacht
And last week soaked a woman's burka with gasoline.

Their sentry caws. Above my house the black
Capes flap the dust out from themselves. The street
Holds still, to wait and listen as they fly off
Trailing the Babel of their squabble and croak.
They raise their children in families, use tools,
And guard each other from the hawk, a few
We've caught of them have almost learned to talk.

Black Autumn

That December evening as I moved
The stack of cedar planks,
With my back to the crisscross pile
I heard the tiny screeching, almost below
My hearing, as if from inside me.
I worked on, filling the cart with boards,
But the shrill sounds kept up,
Rhythmic, like a caught bird.
One of my children pinned somewhere?
His muffled cries a signal in me?
In the still garage, under the glare
Of a single bulb, I strained
For the source of the noise,
Faint and full of terror, then turned
And bent, near the end of my work.
And there at my heel, stretched crooked,
Flat on its back, the stranded creature,
Staring, mouth wide, small teeth bared.
I had torn off—unseeing—its winter sleep
And dropped it broken on the dirt floor.
First I thought to kill it.
Instead, I waited, studied the far off
Voice, the hooked feet almost touching mine.
Then I left it—for any chance it might have—
And walked to the unlit house.
I thought of the cat and dog soon prowling,
Still hearing the bat's call.

Last night, leaving talk in the summer
Evening, I crossed a hill and drifted
In strange country into a stand of old trees,
Birch and maple over deep grass,
And there like shadows bats poured
From the silhouette leaves, dozens
Falling like black autumn

But curling back and dropping again.
One hurled over my shoulder
And I backed toward the path,
But stopped when they turned, swarming
Like waving hands, down to a pond.
Then I followed from behind, flinching
As strays curved around me.
Across the polished water they spread,
Feeding, rising in interlocked circles
And touching their reflections to rings.
I remembered one in winter had strained
To call and that I had left it.
I listened in the rush of these
For a trace of that sound.
Then from the bank, under the first stars,
I entered the reeds and the full churning of wings,
Deaf and tensed against dodging.
Stood still as the fading trees
As they rippled over me
Veering just at my face.
The invisible echoes, the threads
Of their flights fell over my skin,
As out on the water, behind in the woods,
Each of the hundreds turned
On the rudder of its own cry.
I saw in the weave of the bodies
The lines too high for me to hear,
Felt in their close passes
The whispers of absolute location.

Double

Just because I wear a beard
Two women at a bar, neon
With drink and age, won't believe
I'm not Kenny Rogers—
It's so good for somebody
To be there from another world.

And now and again on a dim stair
This: a man catches himself
In mid-sentence talking to me—
"Wait . . . you're not Charlie, are you"—
As what he looked for disappears.

But once a door opened, a woman
I'd never seen began to cry
And wave her hands, staring
Through her fingers at me.
She backed away, then stopped,
And leaned as if to touch. She was
Not young, her hair dyed copper-black.
"Come in," she moaned. Then "I'm sorry,"
Guessing I had come about the car.
She took my arm and led me—
Making the kind of sob that doesn't
Care who hears—down to his room.
All just exactly as he'd left—
The mother's tidiness restrained
Except for dusting—waiting his return.
Tennis shoes slid half under the bed,
His combs, lighter, set of keys
By the mirror she herself stood in.
Twelve years it had been.

Once in a restaurant a waitress cried—
"Go to her" my wife said. I found her
Behind a coat rack, her words buried
In her hands. I was her brother, killed
In Vietnam. And alone again
In the waiting place and asking
If she had faith to get her through.
"In what?" she said, shutting me up,
Making me know myself the stranger,
But strangely certain for her sad love,
That lost brief welcome, that I am.

Diver

> "The last free man in Estonia" was found by
> KGB agents who posed as fishermen.
> —*National Geographic*, 1990

In their file photograph of him, August
Sabe smiles big, threads his slender fly-rod
Beside the rushes he had angled through
The thirty years the Soviets had hunted him,
The last of those who would not leave the woods.
His very line and shoulder bag and grin
Too much to stand, the freedom of his catch.
He tossed one agent in the river, fought
The second till the rest swarmed from the blind.
Like wasps from Satan's ass, he might have joked,
He dived then quick, stroked to the bottom, "hooked
Himself onto a sunken log" and stayed.

The water heavy, cold inside his leather coat,
His hat swept on—it might give him away.
What words had he learned, nights among the stars,
To ready for this act, a hundred ways?
Certain as he hooked the lure into the hide
Of his tough coat and wound the leader fast
Around the trunk long sodden, stirring silt.
The current thickened in his sight, he locked
His legs against its pull, his one breath held.
Like the trees whose roots below the bank
Tap into the river, he drank his words,
And there, the leaves above which fill with light
He filled as well.

                      The ones who did not follow
Stood silent then, were only what they said.
They watched downstream for him. The eider ducks
That dive when shot, clamp roots, will not be taken,
Coasted calmly below their hurried looks.

"The Greatest Generation"
Tom Brokaw, June 6, 1994

My father landed at Normandy,
Slogged through France to Berlin.
Discharged home in '45,
Said nothing of where he'd been.

When my mother opened our door
It was a stranger wearing his grin.
I never once heard him cry
As he went down under his gin.

Other men took to the Trappists,
Vowed silence in a world of sin.
He kept his own *Regula*,
His stories all drowned in him.

The last time he called me he held
A bloody towel to his nose.
Got him cauterized in Emergency—
So much for a lifetime of booze.

Except in a dream once he never
Said goodbye when he left—
His bleeding for now burnt shut,
Then gone, such a grim relief.

On TV—the old men return
To fields where the young men died.
The toughest, asked to remember,
Speak, bite their lips, and cry.

Maybe today he is watching
Those D-Day landings again.
Maybe he's with an old woman
Who guesses where his words begin.

If fifty years later, at last
We all see the corpses in piles,
Learning to talk after war
Takes some soldiers awhile.

Though one night he stood in my dream
As if to say all we missed.
Instead, he reached to me wordless,
Put love on my mouth, one kiss.

Indigo Bunting

The empty county roads I bike first light
Alone, find me the buzzards at their work,
One on a fly-blown possum who still grins.
Into a tight sharp curve, surprise of wings
Flung out, dark, wide, above the blacktop, grace
Of lift and shadow sliding up the trees.
On down the miles, I pass small birds glanced off
In weedy gravel, breast feathers roughed by wind.

Last week I pocketed a small blue bird, still warm,
Took home to show my mother-in-law, my friend,
Her own hands slight and nesting in her lap.
She weighed it lightly, stroked smooth the flaming blue
She had only seen in flashes as she walked.

Down in the bottomland the pastures spread,
A turtle crawls, halfway across the road—
I stop, get off, and hope its compass is set
The way I aim it through a rusty fence.

Back home each day as she grows yet more still
We watch with her, uncertain what to say.
All words into the distance disappear.

On Tunnel Hill just as I make the top
A snake coils on the burning shoulder gravel.
The signal hourglasses of his skin
Make me veer wide, then circle back to look,
Saying *they can only strike as far as their length*.
Flies buzz the head, blood seeps and scabs the dirt,
His skull a wedge, still poised to strike, his slit
Eyes wide and dead. I bend to pick him up
And take him home to show his kind, to warn
The kids, but struck with cold that feels him twist
 Around my arm, spit gleaming in his bite—

You can't hold me even dead and live—I fling
Him out into the field so he won't lure
The other eaters of the dead to death.

I coast on down, a chill at my back, the fangs
I feel yet. I wonder, do I ever help
Or only make a different mess? A flock
Of buntings sweeps from branches overhead,
Then scatters into the tangle of the hedge.

She had smiled, sighed "oh" and "yes" across the body
She studied, iridescent, luminous,
At rest. The assent she gave not sad but from
Far off. That look we see sometimes—someone
Gone deep inside looks out and seems a guest
We had imagined, not known till now. She laid
The bird back in my hand as carefully
As if it were alive, a shock of blue
Split from the light, a body of no weight.

I pedal up a mile-long rise heading home.
A rush of air, a dump truck load of rocks
Slams by. Its wake hauls me, sucks tight my shirt
Against my ribs, breathes dust into my hair.

Choir Boy

i.m. Austin Caswell

We biked out early, far from town, through fields
Of bottomland, green swales of beans and corn.
The sky that backed the hilltops called us on,
You sang "The Ode for St. Cecilia's Day,"
Which claims creation, time itself, is sung.
You said the first you heard of music's power
Was what they taught you, just a boy in choir—
To lift the gathered people up by song
To the threshold of the divine
And hold them there while you looked up, sang on.
Though no one told you how to follow them.

That child you were began an elegy
I couldn't escape—for him, for you and me
Out glad, white-headed, the morning ours to risk
In downhill runs we took too fast, at curves
We leaned into the blindside of, perhaps
To meet each other where heaven begins,
The truck's front end, the crash into light too quick
To shout goodbye. When you got taken for
A slower ride, dead laboring to crank the bike
An hour, we both agreed we wouldn't climb
That hill until we got to it. Last time
We lugged up Shuffle Creek, your blood aflame
With drugs, we made a detour to behold
The grade on Boultinghouse, a rise so cruel
And long you said it made some strong men weep
And joked you used to suffer it once a year
To prove yourself to you. I meant that day
To have a go at it when I still could
Tell you I'd tried. From then, each time we spoke
I listened toward the good farewell, the kind
Men say sometimes before the final fight:
"If we do meet again, why, we shall smile;

If not, why then this parting was well made."
At last you lay too weak to make much talk
But held my hand and let yours speak awhile
For me to hear your silent eloquence
And learn how strong you were becoming weak.

And now it's time, the elegy is due.
Like every death, I can't believe you're gone.
I see you walking up the drive, it's May,
The grass is wet, the bikes are tuned, you tell
A story as we ride off. Perhaps today
You'll sing to teach the power of the voice—
How *The Messiah* begins: out from the dark
Of all humanity strains one long note,
Its rise and fall so pure it's everyone.
Then several more lone calls of heart before
The chorus joins "Oh comfort ye my people,"
Those sounds that even if we've never heard
God's name will take us to the *threshold of*
The place you called *divine* a lifetime back
And sang toward to lift the others there.
We're sure: of time there's never enough, and yet—

Here I imagine you among the boys
White surpliced rows in choir, your hair slicked down,
Tones clear as innocence, pitched high and sharp
Against the ceiling of the nave where you
Watch singing to see if they've reached heaven yet—

Whenever I'm out riding I pray for you
For whenever in your life you needed prayer.
It may be me old man, to you a boy—
For who knows how or where?
Alone in morning on the bike, in joy,
For when I need it, Austin, send one too.

2

Speak that I may know thee.
—BEN JONSON

The Deal

A word can heal, a word can slit a throat.
My uncle came home once cut ear to ear.
He'd quarreled with a stranger whose razor spoke.

I didn't see his sticky shirt wrapped tight—
Though I was very young I learned to hear—
Around his neck. His skin my mother said,

And she was just a girl, had gone chalk white,
His eyes blinked wide, rolled blind back in his head.
We're made of memory. They got the doc

To stitch him shut, no cops, they cut a deal.
The one who laid him open they paid back.
Whatever happens happens to us all.

I had to find another way to talk.
My mother stayed up late at night and read.
Years later he found a worse way to be dead.

Supper

It's not I couldn't forgive, I can't forget,
The afternoon—my heart still gripped on this—
There was no food at all, he took the six
Of us and with the few green dollars we had
Bought peanut butter and a loaf of bread
And beer, and then at the kitchen table spread
(The only time he ever made us supper)
The stuff so thin it made me hungrier
To see our lives left in a tiny jar,
And what this is (I taste it now) is hate,
The little girls still stand around the table, wait
(Although he drank us up, he was the father)
For me to kill him, love be a murderer.
I couldn't swallow death then and cannot yet.

Once His Hand

Once his hand, tough and thick,
Cradled my forehead as I puked black—
Somewhere in me leaking blood,
My appendix ruptured.
So wrung out I'd fouled my hair,
Left alone, slid to the floor,
The retching let me—eleven—
Rest myself against him then.

This once the poison said I must
Hang there in the hand that struck
Just yesterday when I ducked past
And knocked the stars into the black
Behind my eyes—that fist
Now open as my body twisted
Out the long tight last
Of me and then went slack.

Once like this, I could be held,
Limp and wet as the sheets I soiled—
Fading, the imprint on my skull
The one thing I could tell.

Muse

Shale. Mud. The sky skidded down
The spilled slag of mountains. Tamaracks,
Stunted sycamores. Floating grackles,
Green-black as bruises, that clattered
Over the hollow. A caved-in barn, shacks,
'50 Pontiac wrecked in the creek bed.
I'd volunteered, come down to help.

You waited there, surprised me, woman,
With belief. So gaunt I could not work
In your stare, afraid of being haunted.
Like the yellow-eyed thing with fur
That skulked under the slab of rock.
The Mission's shelter torched, a cop
Seen there before a crop was busted.
But your voice took me where you wanted.

Those words, iron twang of loss, cut soft
Ideas of beauty out. Around here, you said,
Some preach not to carry a gun,
Sin of presumption against
The Providence of God. The dead of March,
The hard clay under us toward thaw,
You showed me where I'd sleep, steel bed,
Old mattress to unroll.

                        Outside, your work,
Straw bale cold-frame flocked with snow,
Salvaged window sashes across the top, frost
Thick, you brushed away for me to see—
Sprouts that begged scant living from the sun.

Your bare hand grazed mine, more than a kiss
Cracked skin told how hope was kept,
A lust of promise, starved, clean, yourself.

I could not talk, entered your look,
Survival along stone dark water
Of the ruined runoff creek, your hard
Faith author of the sprouts half frozen
Each night below the glass, that green
Licked up to light, your gardened land
Too hard to take a seed, that rose in me.
Forgetting reasons I had come, then close,
Your mouth my mouth, "You have to choose"
Your voice in me "to stay alive."

Kingfisher

Stuttering screech and a blue streak
Tears over the pond or down the creek.
One thing he doesn't do is sneak,
Lights on a branch, death in his beak.

Of Soldiers and Others

Peace hath her victories no less renowned than war
—MILTON, "SONNET ON GENERAL CROMWELL," 1652

Of soldiers, one in five will shoot to kill
The generals say—though any of the five
Can die. While all are firing at will,
I see the eye, the steady hand survive,

And rise a crack above the barricade,
And with the firm imagination of
The bullet in the other's head unmade,
He holds his breath and squeezes as in love.

It's clear why Cromwell's army never lost
For every man of his meant what he shot—
Was glad to die if that was what life cost—
Because he aimed at what he really thought.

The heart unfocused fires and takes a dive.
But loving what it loves—just one in five.

Box of Ashes

They brought a box of ashes to the wake,
A stillborn child we hadn't known about,
When John the drunkard she was married to
Had knocked her down the steps. Who is to blame
That she had given herself to such a man?
My father surely who taught her this was love.
And what of him—all guilty? all excused?—
Abandoned by his father at two weeks old,
That man an Irish immigrant, the son
Himself of a Republican beat near
To death inside a British jail, kicked out
To die. Her body was being cremated
That very hour, next day the burial.
He handed us the box, its secret date—
For twenty years she'd taken it every move.
And now we had to get it in the grave
With her despite the cemetery's rules.
It's always down to sin and love, to give
Or not good answer to a voice's call.
How did we learn how she had lost the child?
Her daughter, just nine back then, had heard it all.
Which makes us pray a prayer right now could stretch
Back to the moment she was almost falling out of reach.

Honesty

The pond was dug out thirty years ago,
A few bass, sunfish, some crappies released.
On its own it took in copperheads, frogs,
Catfish, carp, softshells, and the snapping jaws
That keep the wild ducks off from underneath.
At last it got so thick that just the ugliest
And most mouthed best survived. Algae- and reed-
Clogged, cattailed, silt-clouded—slick and mud-cauled
Whatever was dragged out or slithered up.

Late summer the stink hung intestinal.
We had to drain it down to half and shock
It three times with sufficient drug to kill
Whatever lived below and breathed that stuff.
Rough-fish no one could believe the size of
Bellied up, the surface scaled with the glut.
We raked the corpses off, and stunned it good
A second day. The bodies floated up, surprised—
One bass, so big we thought it was a dream.

The third day when the death went in it all
Went dead, but one old snapping turtle I'd forgot,
Had dumped in when I thought anything would do.
It crawled up like a great goddamn, spike-rimmed,
Plates-dripping, drunk—stretched out its snaky neck
Just long enough to get its head whacked off.
My uncle picked it up by its hind legs
And said "good eating if the pond was clean."
Out of its stump blood dripped as red as mine.

I jammed a stick, as if it knew me, its beak
Clamped shut.

Late Winter Night

For my aged mentor, friend

Your street become a wilderness,
Your hair unraveled, a broken nest
You peek through looking madly lost,
Your words directed to some ghost
I do not see,
Though he draws near with cold hints of
What once was you with me,
A specter made of what was love.

The child you searched for, called, bereft,
Has disappeared into the drifts.
I take your hand to lead you now
From where you've fallen soaked with snow,
Bent low and empty into your house,
Stained money, garbage, scattered about.
You cannot tell
Me where you've been, yet still we speak,
My voice trying to cross the spell
That in your dream you may awake.

We find your bed, no sheets, food-smeared,
I ease you into the end I feared,
You scowl at me, then shut your eyes,
It is your face, though in disguise.
Your mind all trees, uncomforted,
I will not think you better off dead
But cover you
With your fur coat, now ripped and matted,
With the prayers for me you must have said,
And try to un-knot your frozen shoe.

The Fall

A bird no bigger than a leaf flies up
Unsinging through a woods of shedding leaves,
The one heart thought I must believe
Against the endless-seeming drop
Of all that grieve.

Prophet

If you can split a crow's tongue
You can teach him to talk.

Take him from the high nest
Before he's fledged out full.
Then keep him clipped
Till he's all black silk,
Feathers stiff for flight
And hops at you like
He wants you to know something.
Pull a nylon stocking over him,
Tie his wrinkled feet together,
Have someone with hard fingers
Hold his head firm
So he can't jerk back.
Cork his beak open
Till a single-edged razor
Fits in against his tongue.
If he doesn't do the job himself,
Flip his gullet once,
And what you see just then
In the black bead of his eye is

The shock of a fixed
Heart breaking toward talk.

Snake Handlers

I have to admire at least one thing
Of snake-handlers, however wrong
Or short their sight.
They take the deadly sting
Rather than risk life stupid *and* long.

Stoplight

> To the man with the "Homeless and Hungry" sign.

I don't care whether you are or aren't a fake.
You've got a face, I've got a buck.
Whatever makes you stand here—Jesus—I
Wouldn't trade you luck for luck.
You say "God bless you, brother" as you take
The thin green touch that slips between
Us as the light—I catch your eye—stays red.
Then you step back, the glass that slides up ends
Whoever you are or what your blessing means.
Compassion is—the light turns green,
Wherever you will sleep tonight
The underpass or Christian flophouse bed—
A better fate than being right.
We have to find for Jesus' sake
The best way to die broke,
Brief friend,
Before we're dead.

Why Tom Kalen Rode the Bulls, and The Mystery of the First Commandment

He clenched his teeth into a grin
He never gave up as he snapped *Open it*
And jammed his heels in to make it buck—
Go fuck yourself if you think he would quit—
He "came to play" the eight seconds that he had
To stay hung on the bolting spine and ribs,
To take the jolt, to rise up on the ton that lurched
And shook to slam him off, to ride the twist,
And fly feet down, not flinch and risk neck break,
Not trip but hit the dirt—an ex-
Marine just home from Vietnam—and roll,
Eyes sharp, out from the thud of hooves, the horns
Untipped, not get hammered, gored—stand quick,
Pick up his hat, slap off the dust and not
Look back.
           In a game film once when I had scored,
Coach ran it backward, forward, just counting him
Again, again, in one play throw three blocks.
He stuck the noseguard, slid off, cleaned out
The weakside backer as I cut, then caught
The safety coming over, left each one flat.
Reversed, we watched and watched him throw himself
Into each downed man to rack him up
Onto his feet. Jesus, God, who made and kept
The first commandment—whole heart, soul, mind, and strength—
You must have loved him clear through death,
For if he never crossed himself or knelt,
He looked straight in the eye of the one he got,
Climbed on, smiled, and clenched the deal.

3

He saw a man named Matthew . . . and he
said to him, "Follow me."
—MATTHEW 9:9

St. Matthew and the Angel

To my children

Though you're not here with me, I wish you here.
Before the moment of this gilt-leaf frame,
Enough to hold a more than life-sized man,
Two figures, close-ups, at work inside of it—

The center of the painting, the man's left hand
Arched lightly on his chest above his heart.
The fingers rest below his beard, feel for
The notes on some imagined instrument.

Upper left behind his shoulder, the angel—
Its eyes thick-browed, wide open, staring love,
Almost with adoration in their kindness—
Breathes at his ear, lips slightly pursed to mouth
Exactly, even pursed a little to its left
And down to aim the whisper to his heart.

The lower edge: the man's right hand, his pen
Point on the page, about to scratch a word,
The book already old, his gesture one
A tax collector might have made, the coins
Bagged, inked, ready for the next in line.

But here St. Matthew looks above our heads
Into the distance, thinking hard. The angel's word
Is taking shape beneath the cloak's deep folds,
The Master's face again within the dark which floods
This scene, the twist of cloth that binds his hair,
The ridges of his beard, the hinted room
Whose details, lost in shadow, we can feel.

Now seen up close enough to touch, his sight
Is paint, his eyes so many layers of black,
His look arises, living, out of them.

The angel, both a woman and a man
And more than one has laid its light-struck hand
So gently on the human shoulder that
It feels the power imagination is,
His love, his Lord again, the Dutch canal,
The Lake, outside the windowed studio,
Of Galilee, the Babel of the crowds
Now stilled, the voice of God inside the sound
Of Jesus saying *the Kingdom of Heaven is*. . . .

Beneath the textured brushstrokes of the eyes,
The sunken skin, the cheekbones of the saint,
The canvas cracks spread yet a deeper age,
Thread through the face as time keeps curing it.
Is death the last word days can say to us?
Or just the first? This near, the messenger
Has come to kiss, speaks slow for words to search
The regions of the memories he is.

This solid spirit which the man can only know
By what he dreams is tinged with light for us.
It casts its shadow where it lays its hand
And where it leans into the hair and time-
Dark aura of the man. We realize
Ourselves that it is studying its way
Into the vanishing point within his chest.
The deep connections of the vision here
Emerge, composed, all lines directed by
The light. From any angle at which we stand
Reality is what the angel says.

The light, high left, shines down across the bodies
Onto the book below. We are not shown
Its source, or rays of thin gold lines from God
That strike consent in other imagined rooms,

But see it lively, glancing along the fringes
Of the angel's coppery hair, onto the temple
Of the man, his burnished ear. It draws
Illumination from within each face
Just slightly turned to profile, and from the burning hand
That rests, keeps count upon his chest. On down,
Along the folded shadows of the robe
The light suggests by barely touching it,
Then pools in the waiting pages below.
There light-filled oils create the vellum, lifting
Edges layered like mother-of-pearl. The hand
That waits to write, a knot caught in the glow.

The angel, working, loves him more and more,
Its joy deepening joy embracing all—
The upper hand, old veined as rocks, big knuckled,
Adam risen to hear his grave-worn name,
To feel—testily—for words formed in his throat,
The ready lower hand, as heavy as mud,
One finger broken that holds the upraised pen
Into the book that rests upon the frame.

The right half of the scene is dark, a room
We have to guess. As I stay to listen, the old
Stand long and watch, the young pass quickly on.
I see yet closer into that lightless part,
Discover letters, stroked long and elegant,
Ends scrolled as finely as a violin's neck—
Rembrandt, a purer black in black, so deep
It's only visible in angled sight.
Then *1661*, in yet more dark
Emblazoned on the half-imagined wall,
Its measure of light the least before no light.

Stand close and look across from right to left,

Your own head just below their lines of vision.
From sight comes yet more sight, the angel's face
Made strange by its delight, the feel of
Itself within a heart, the secret work,
The place no one can go, save God. The shock
Held in the angel's eyes bleeds in the dark
Hair of the man, whose suffering fills all
He sees, love steady in his stare which looks
Above our heads to Israel, to time
Reborn into Gethsemane, Christ's hands
And feet. The angel is kissing him, I swear.

The light, how it recedes as I step back,
Returns, more vibrant when I near.
The canvas, now I see better still, not cracked
But ridged and clotted with the earthlike paint,
His finger not broken as I thought but curved
Against the pen, its body one quick stroke.
The slash of white left by the tip so fine
The hairs are countable, and like the angel
Composed of light and nothing—full bodied being
Slight, mixed color and white laid on lip wet.

How young, full mouthed the angel, how worn, hurt,
The man. Wherever the rest of this heavenly spirit
Abides, its head and its right hand arise
Just over the shoulder, barely in the frame,
Un-haloed, wingless, otherworldly, slipped in
Beside the pain-furrows of the forehead, cheeks,
The wincing crevices of the eyes, their glint.
The angel's voice shivers in the spell of light,
The words the man is living and will write,
The model for the spirit the artist's son,
The heavenly human image of the man
Divine, at once grown old and young again.

The page he is about to pen lifts up,
In motion, impatient to be filled and turn.
What is the limit of what we're here to learn?

I turn back as I leave—across the room,
Its high walls, emptiness, a few who drift
Awhile still before the doors are locked.
The angel seen from here, now distancing,
Must be a lover or a dream come close.
Its presence sudden, the man is on alert,
A voice he recognizes before it's heard
Is lifting him, his face becoming light.

I look again. At those still musing here
The last half hour. At you within my heart
And far away. At this, Rembrandt's configuring us,
The man who even when the lights go out,
When imagination only fills the room,
Writes down the story the messenger is giving.
At the angel's rare expression—I did not know
We could be loved so much—as it says
Exactly what it can into each ear.

4

But thou shalt have a perfect and just weight,
a perfect and just measure shalt thou have.
—DEUTERONOMY 25:15

I'm Fine

"I'm fine" she said and died.
At first, we thought she lied.

Bloomington Landfill, 14 Degrees

A flock of white-winged gulls kaleidoscope,
Rising, falling in a wheel of cries
Along a newly bulldozed precipice
Where garbage trucks back in and dump.

Their hungers sweep and hover above my head
As I heave trash out over this brink, this dust
And light in motion, eyes blinking out the grit,
My hands half frozen, feet slipping on the grime.

A junk-filled pickup crowds to get my place,
I cannot stop, long watch these birds, their grace
Ride gusts that snap the torn plastic bags
And tumble rags away across the stink

As lightly as they did the offshore wind
Where I first saw their flights along the beach—
A boy alone, they, messengers that screed
And swooped across the edge of all I guessed.

Sky salt and wet, the backwash hissing down
The gleaming sand, they spoke of what must be,
But not yet, understood. Their bodies memory
As much the first time seen as now, like love.

Among the waste, the towering dives, the rush,
To have to say goodbye, to need to touch.

Intention

Mark 5:27

To touch the hem of his garment
She bends low
And all his God into her fingers flows.
What she meant he meant
Flooding her body flooding her soul.

The Sheep and the Goats

Matthew 25:36

She got my number, asked for a ride to jail.
She leaves her child out on the walk to wait
With others waving, looking up. Sometimes
The women bare their breasts. She wouldn't do that.
She's overweight, hair slick, and waits in line
To talk, a square of scratched up plexiglass,
A wire-mesh mouthpiece under it—if I
Didn't believe the Gospel I'd never come
Myself—part of his face, sharp eyes, dark smile,
Her mouth then ear up close. The promise is
He's waiting there for us to visit Him.
She listens to this one she didn't know
Till he was caged up here say *Sweetheart, Baby,*
Whatever it takes to squeeze a buck from her.
I meet the one I've volunteered to help
Go straight when he gets to the halfway house.
Their voices trickle through the boiler plate,
His body crooked on the other side,
She'll wear his bruises herself when he's released.
I've known her with her different faces, names—
She never owns a car, and I believe
Her when she says she cares for him. Her need
Is hell, with no escape for anyone but love.
I take her where the promises begin,
Where I keep going for now, though I won't know—
He says this in the parable—it's Him.
Then take her home, see her again, again.

Keeping In Sight

At first I try to not imagine hells
On earth, the prison cell of 8 x 12
You're locked in with a man who's crazy mean.
But then I go to visit you, to learn
The razor wire wound over ten-foot spikes,
The body search, the taking off my belt,
The clank of shunting through escape-proof locks,
Then you across the table in prison clothes.
The guard says "Keep your hands in sight." You smile
And hold them out palms up. It's your same face,
Your voice, your look. But as I hear you rap
About your chance for early out, the case
For what is real or deadly hope, your eyes
Give up. At every pause, the words run dry.
A pain burns through your sight so deep you squint
Until you find the next good thing to say.
I listen closely so I learn to pray
And you keep one eye open while you sleep.

Blue Note Lounge, Face-off

For B. W.

New cop, told me he'd follow Christ,
Would shoot to kill. Saw the lightning flash
Of fear in, unredeemed, the eyes
That looked in his, the other gun
Snout up. The choice jumpy in
The hand—that quick, a squeeze, a jolt
Inside the skin—no thought.
Under his jacket the metal vest—
"Drop it." "Now." He prayed the words
Would work. Each body in the room held
One short judgment breath. His soul,
His credibility strung out between
The two of them, the aims they'd fixed.
He read the angle, knew he'd get
It in the vest, fire off a round
At least and take him out.
His three last words, his finger tight,
Died from the frozen crowd. He watched
The lips compressed, jaw clenched on what
They each were having to accept—
To work an out before the shot—
While he was counting in his head
To five, all he had left to give.
He wanted not to kill him but he would,
His shirt so thin across, outside, his chest,
Like the boy he, once, had been, unsure,
Pushed by the words he'd said, the taunts
The shadows all around them held,
Who might still be afraid to move
To lay it down. But then
At *four*, he did.
The cop remembered later, in that next breath,
Stale beer stink as he put him down to cuff,

The wrists so thin without the gun, the scar
Keloid down one of them, the mirror behind
The bar in which he rose and saw himself
Himself.

City Hospital, June Night

With just a scent, a name, I am again
Beside the bed my cousin Leigh died in,
The brown block walls, the dimmed, post-op room light,
The wrapping around her damaged head all white,
The girl face so beautiful and bruised
Asleep, her silence that our breath abused
To see her there about to leave the *why*
Without a way to speak or hear *goodbye*.

Again again, all love I did not say.
I put my hand upon her hand to stay,
Before the gray seeps in her cheeks, my mind.
Not let these eyes, not let the heart, go blind.
Is time beginning or is it just an end?
The comfort of the Resurrection?—when
Christ holds me to her slowly numbing skin.

Christmas Weather Report

> The weather is: CLEAR AND FAIR
> The next holiday is: CHRISTMAS
> —SIGN SEEN IN A NURSING HOME

They never know outside weather, only
The dead air fluorescent lit and the hum
Of the ventilators in the lonely
Room. Better to die quick, I think, a bum
In the scrub woods beside the railroad track
In the cold dark sky as the brain goes numb.

Past where the road stops, in a windy shack,
No longer a path to it, so weathered
No one, even if he did see it, would go back.
Sun and rain, the mostly indifferent birds.
To be old waiting there, peaceful and dumb,
For Christ to come.

Diagnosis

If you should see me fading out, she said,
And cannot keep my gaze in yours, tell me
To go ahead, that you'll be there to see
Me coming to the shore, and I'll be led.
If you should touch me and I do not turn
To find the guiding of your hands, fold mine
Into each other, press them for a sign
Of patience in the silence we will learn.
Can you regard me with no answering smile?
Without the kindly tone of voice that says
What in the absence from you my heart prays?
Will you believe I'm somewhere for that while?
Inside that moment when I don't return
Your word—if love holds then it holds unearned.

To My Wife Caring for Her Parents Far from Here

This time apart let loneliness be prayer,
Let joy in its saddest mien awake,
As you go mourning in the morning air.

The sun wakes me, I feel you rising there
And listening at their door, their breath, their ache—
This time apart let loneliness be prayer.

You help them dress, help comb their thinning hair,
You let the light into the time they take,
As you go mourning in the morning air.

They move so slow they almost disappear
And take you with them, but love's no mistake.
This time apart let loneliness be prayer.

They fast until the Eucharist you share,
Their meal itself as small, on tongues that shake,
As you go mourning in the morning air.

I dream you in your hour alone, out where
You run among the graves so you won't break,
So time apart lets loneliness be prayer
So you go, morning, in the mourning air.

Blue Nightgown

My wife slips through the room, where I read late,
To close the windows. Her blue silk's whispering
Trails out into the tight-strung voices of the spring
That rise a moment, then seal off, that state

The book had held me in, a dream. The light
Above my head the last, from half shadow
She returns, then closely in its single glow
Leans toward me in the gown of this full night.

At once I feel this time the only left
Of all those early ones we carried here
Or that carried us, or that we were and wear.
Her face light-blessed, so near, I am bereft

Of words, so many hours of us gone.
A moth beats in the lampshade its moment long,
The mantle clock we bought when young strikes home,
She kisses me, looks in my eyes. I'm stunned

To touch her present hand, the works it's done.
Good night, alone in silence. *Good night*, a song.

County Clare

Deep in the hilly field the wedge grave shone—
Sunken table stones, the slant roof slab
Still high enough for a man to walk straight in.
Nearby, a herd grazed, spread down from the ridge.
She stayed while I walked out, testing for bog,
Eyeing the cows to be sure I was right,
Could see what I was out there with. Halfway,
Mike, I heard, then *Mike*, but nothing else,
Unsure in the stillness it was her voice.
I stopped, and then, *Look right.* There on a rise
I had not seen, hid by shadow—head up,
The neck and shoulders massed, the thick brass ring
His signature—he stood to see who crossed
His field. The cows cleared off between the grave
And me, hooves gouging muck. I moved from tuft
To tuft, mud sucking down my feet, so slow
I could see his eyes see mine. A drawn-out moan
Called for a calf to come away. I must
Not run but make it to the stones. I could
Not see her then but went on faith, the bull
Still watching as I crossed the threshold dirt.
In shade inside the monoliths I asked
Myself where I was now—this rough-cut dolman
Urged up four thousand years ago, these calves
Gathered big-eyed, the clay dried in their coats,
To stare in through the gaps, the dirt floor hollowed,
Sifted, grave-robbed, millennia ago,
Even the bones placed there long pillaged.
The bull had drifted, grazing. I looked for her.
Above, on the brink of the field, just at a break
In the hedge, her body small in the wet-struck light,
She had not screamed at me *Run for your life*
But with a quieting instinct knew she must
As Patrick Carey later would tell us
Not, by God, excite them no matter what.

I waited to escape and as I brushed
The walls I half could feel their rising once
By mystery and sweat—a place to hide
Whatever one of us must have to cross
To where the dead go leaving us.
Too far away to call, I looked toward her
Watching, holding—for my return—that voice
I heard her send my name in over me.
Then silence, then my name, *Look right,* again.

Maggie

I woke into the sounds of your bad dream,
Reached to your warmth, touched you, and softly said
It's okay, Maggie, I'm here, you're in your bed.
Your murmurs slowed, you shifted toward me, seemed

To say my name, then quieted again,
Breathed deep away, my comfort mine to keep.
Not wanting you to lose your thread of sleep,
I kept my kiss, but needed to kiss you then

But would not call you back from your safe place
And caught the panic of Eurydice—
That you would go before I let you see
The dying of my heart to touch your face.

You slept away—I knew forever I
Would learn how far off death is when you die.

Just Weight

The oak logs frozen in the lean-to shed
Clunk down upon the block and stand on end.

The baby cries and twists around some pain,
I stand with him, his back against my ribs.

The wood has dried a year, unknotted, clean,
I tap one chunk with the axe to test its grain.

We rock from side to side; I hum his name
To catch his rhythm, ride it in my own.

At just one hit the first round splits, so neat
The halves knock down in two clean widths.

Each tilt and turn I sway I feel his squalls
Upcaught; he gives up arching, stops his kick.

I stack the heartwood logs into the grate,
Leave space for flames to leap, sunlight released.

As if he hears my wish pulse into him,
His squirming calms, his breath slips into dream.

He sleeps on me as I sink down to rest
His body just love's weight upon my chest.

The Keeper's Voice

John 3:27

I felt the sound begin when just a boy
Up in the dark, hot coffee in my gut,
Swung open the pasture gate beside the barn,
Stepped farther into chill, thick sodden grass,
Low mist, a few leftover stars that watched.
Among the clouds that split across the sky
I felt my way still higher, climbed the fence
And perched upon the corner post, breathed deep
The distance of the house, the city so far.
Into this close and shifting hold of dark
Called long and low as Bob had taught me to
The milking cry the cows lost in the field
Understood, not words but almost words,
The tone as otherworldly as I could make,
Sik caalf, sik caalf, hi yup, hi yup, sik caalf
And then their human names worked in, *Big Red
Hi yup, hi yup Daisy, Shorty, hi up Bess.*
Over the hill of the field I watched, no thought
Of what the words once were that warped to this,
Long conversation between the cows and men
That I, just ten, became the mystery of
Again, soliloquy of sounds I trolled
Across the emptiness, becoming just
A voice until at last the bodies hulked
Slow, shadowed, one by one, still made of dark
Strung out. Then in the gathering herd I felt
Not saw—*Sik caalf, Brownie, hi yup, hi yup*—
The udders tight, in sway, the drips of milk.
A long moan answers, rising in our talk.